NEW MEXICO'S CHACO CANYON

Also by James C. Wilson from Sunstone Press:

Hiking New Mexico's Chaco Canyon: The Trails, The Ruins, The History
Santa Fe, City of Refuge: An Improbable Memoir of the Counterculture

The Fernando Lopez Santa Fe Mystery Series:

Peyote Wolf
Smokescreen
Ghost Canyon
The Dead Go Fast
Painted Skull Ranch
Devil on Canyon Road
Taos Gothic
Taos Vendetta

NEW MEXICO'S CHACO CANYON

Photographing the Ancient City
A companion to *Hiking New Mexico's Chaco Canyon*

JAMES C. WILSON

SUNSTONE PRESS
SANTA FE

© 2023 by James C. Wilson
All Rights Reserved
No part of this book may be reproduced in any form or by any electronic or mechanical means including information storage and retrieval systems without permission in writing from the publisher, except by a reviewer who may quote brief passages in a review.

Sunstone books may be purchased for educational, business, or sales promotional use. For information please write: Special Markets Department, Sunstone Press, P.O. Box 2321, Santa Fe, New Mexico 87504-2321.
Printed on acid-free paper
∞

Library of Congress Cataloging-in-Publication Data

Names: Wilson, James C., 1948- author.
Title: New Mexico's Chaco Canyon : photographing the ancient city : a companion to "Hiking New Mexico's Chaco Canyon" / James C. Wilson.
Other titles: Photographing the ancient city : a companion to "Hiking New Mexico's Chaco Canyon"
Description: Santa Fe : Sunstone Press, [2023] | Includes bibliographical references. | Summary: "New Mexico's Chaco Canyon: Photographing the Ancient City is a guide to photographing the monumental stone city, including advice on where, when, and sometimes how to photograph, with detailed information about the history of the Chaco culture with map and a collection of the author's photographs"-- Provided by publisher.
Identifiers: LCCN 2023030785 | ISBN 9781632935458 (paperback)
Subjects: LCSH: Chaco Culture National Historical Park (N.M.)--Tours. | Chaco Culture National Historical Park (N.M.)--Pictorial works. | Landscape photography--New Mexico--Chaco Culture National Historical Park.
Classification: LCC F802.C4 W55 2023 | DDC 779.478982--dc23
LC record available at https://lccn.loc.gov/2023030785

WWW.SUNSTONEPRESS.COM
SUNSTONE PRESS / POST OFFICE BOX 2321 / SANTA FE, NM 87504-2321 /USA
(505) 988-4418

Entry fees, campground fees and rules, as well as other rules regarding times and dates quoted here are based on information at the time of this book's publication and may change. Visitors to Chaco should check the Chaco Culture National Historical Park website for updated information.

National Park Service Map of Chaco Canyon

CONTENTS

Preface: Photographing with Respect / 10
Introduction / 11
A Quick Overview of Chaco and its History / 13

Gallo Campground / 16
    Stop No. 1: Red Pictograph
    Stop No. 2: Overlook Trail

Downtown Chaco / 22
    Stop No. 3: Pueblo Bonito
    Stop No. 4: Chetro Ketl

North Mesa / 32
    Stop No. 5: Kin Kletso
    Stop No. 6: Pueblo Bonito Overlook
    Stop No. 7: Pueblo Alto
    Stop No. 8: Chetro Ketl Overlook
    Stop No. 9: Canyon Overlook

West Mesa / 43
    Stop No. 10: Petroglyph Panels
    Stop No. 11: Supernova Pictograph
    Stop No. 12: Peñasco Blanco
    Stop No. 13: The Convergence of the Chaco and Escavada Washes
    Stop No. 14: Casa Rinconada

South Mesa / 52
    Stop No. 15: The Chaco Meridian
    Stop No. 16: Tsin Kletsin

Wijiji and Chacra Mesa / 56
    Stop No. 17: Chaco Wash
    Stop No. 18: Wijiji

After the Fall: A short History / 60
Recommended Reading / 64

Preface: Photographing With Respect

Chaco Culture National Historical Park is a UNESCO World Heritage Site. Please show respect when you hike and photograph at Chaco, not only because the Antiquities Act makes it a crime to destroy or steal antiquities, but because the Hopi, Zuni, Acoma and other Pueblos consider Chaco their ancestral homeland. The canyon is a sacred place, a spiritual center and symbol of migration valued by all New Mexicans. So please, don't destroy or deface any of the ruins or remove any objects from the park. Let's all commit to a humble, gentle way of being in the world and in doing so preserve our heritage.

Introduction

In *Hiking New Mexico's Chaco Canyon* I wrote a trail guide based on my nearly fifty years of hiking and camping in Chaco Canyon. I intend this book to be a companion volume of sorts. Here I offer advice and write about my experiences photographing Chaco Canyon, including the ruins, the ancient roads, and the wider landscape. There is so much to see and photograph that you could spend days photographing in the canyon and on the mesa trails and still not have exhausted the possibilities. The canyon can be intimidating, offering one visual treasure after another, all of which makes it difficult to explore in one day--or even two days if you choose to camp at Chaco's Gallo Campground. That means visitors must carefully manage their time in the park. To that end, this book includes tips for amateur photographers on where--and in some cases when and how--to find and photograph the major attractions at Chaco.

Chaco Culture National Historical Park is a World Heritage site located in Northwest New Mexico where Ancestral Puebloans built a monumental stone city twelve hundred years ago. That city, nestled in Chaco Canyon, served as the center of a trading empire that reached as far south as Mesoamerica and as far west as the coast of California. We know this because of the cacao and macaw feathers, the seashells and the precious stones found in the ruins of the twelve Great Houses in the canyon. The Chacoan empire lasted from about 850 to 1200 A.D. The reasons for its fall remain as mysterious as the canyon itself. Extreme drought, social unrest, political malaise, invaders from the north, all have been suggested as possible reasons for the fall of what Stephen Lekson in *The Chaco Meridian* calls the "Pax Chaco." Today, eight hundred years later, the canyon remains with its rugged beauty and its spectacular ruins that have the timeless quality shared by other ancient ruins, the pyramids of Egypt or Machu Picchu, for example.

When I'm at Chaco with my camera, I feel like a kid in a candy store. Even though I've been coming here for decades, I still find visual gems that I've not seen before or simply overlooked. You have to remember that the sky and the light are constantly changing in the canyon. A photo of a particular ruin will change depending on conditions at the time you select. Cloudy days are particularly interesting because of the shadows they create. The shadows seem to dance on the walls of the stone ruins and produce intriguing patterns on the sandstone cliffs that line the canyon. Overcast days are my least favorite, because they leave the Great Houses dark and dreary looking, whereas on sunny days they come alive. Fortunately, New Mexico is famous for its clear skies and transcendent light. Over the last one hundred years the New Mexico light has attracted hundreds, if not thousands of painters and photographers, including myself.

Two things I want to point out at the beginning. First, you don't need to be a professional photographer to take spectacular photos of Chaco Canyon. Second, you don't need to have an expensive camera to take spectacular photos of Chaco Canyon. Personally, I generally use a moderately priced Nikon 7200, which suits me just fine. For long photos of the canyon or the ruins, I use a Nikkor 18-140 mm 1:35-5.6 lens. Up close or inside the Great Houses, I use two fixed Nikkor lenses to get sharper images: a 35 mm 1:1.8 lens, and a 50 mm 1:1.8 lens. You can judge the results on the coming pages.

Note: some new model cell phone cameras take excellent photos, which are perfectly fine for personal or online social media use, but not for enlargement or reproduction. I would recommend at least an 18 megapixel camera for these uses. Most of the top brand DSLR cameras can match or exceed this benchmark.

My first chapter offers a quick overview of Chaco Canyon. The remainder of the book divides into geographic sections that, when followed, provides a continuous and hopefully leisurely path through Chaco Canyon. Each section includes stops for photo opportunities that I've found especially advantageous. I start at Gallo Campground and then proceed to Downtown Chaco on the floor of the canyon. From there we go to sites on the North Mesa Trail; the West Mesa Trail; the South Mesa Trail; and finally to the Wijiji Trail.

For more of my work, check out my Author's Page on Amazon and my two Facebook Pages, Southwest Images and Southwest Writings.

A Quick Overview of Chaco and Its History

One thousand years ago greater Chaco Canyon was a bustling metropolis of anywhere from two to twenty thousand inhabitants, with Great Houses and underground kivas built of sandstone masonry equal to anything built today. The Chacoans worked extensive fields, with dams and canals to irrigate their crops, including maize, beans, and squash. They built Great Kivas and large communal plazas for public functions as well as roads, some as wide as thirty feet, that extended out in every direction like tentacles reaching out to collect traders and nomadic hunter-gatherers from the Southern or Midwestern plains. Along the primary artery, the Great North Road, they built fire towers in a line-of-sight communication system that allowed them to communicate with northern outliers at places like Aztec Ruin, New Mexico, and Chimney Rock in Southern Colorado.

At Chaco Canyon Ancestral Puebloans traded with Navajo, Ute, Apache, and other tribes from the North and East. But Chaco Canyon was also an important ceremonial center, where religious ceremonies and rituals were performed throughout the year at times that were keyed to both the solar and lunar calendars. In fact, scholars have shown that virtually all the Great Houses in the canyon are aligned to either solar or lunar events.

Several hundred years before Chaco Canyon emerged as an urban center, the inhabitants of the canyon lived in pit houses and were part of what is called the Basketmaker Culture. About 800 A.D. something dramatic occurred that enabled Chaco to become the preeminent regional power by about 900 AD. Possibly the transformative spark was provided by new building techniques imported from Mesoamerica, and/or the arrival of powerful clans that became the ruling elite of Chaco, sometimes called the *altepetl*.

Chaco Canyon's Great Houses tell the story. Construction of Pueblo Bonito, Peñasco Blanco, and Una Vida began around 850. Chetro Ketl,

Pueblo Alto, Hungo Pavi, and Casa Rinconada started about 1000–1027, Pueblo del Arroyo about 1075. The five other Great Houses were constructed in the first three decades of the 12th century: Wijiji, Tsin Kletsin, Kin Kletso, Casa Chiquita, and New Alto. By 1150 there were over thirty major outliers, Chaco-style Great Houses built in regional or satellite communities as far west as Canyon de Chelly, as far north as Chimney Rock, as far East as Pueblo Pintado, and as far south as the Guadalupe Ruin.

The walls of the ancient buildings were built with sandstone mined from the cliffs of the canyon, chipped and fitted into place using a core-and-veneer construction, with the core being a mix of mud and rubble between the interior and exterior walls. The precision of the fitted stonework seems like a metaphor for the culture's interdependent relationship with the natural world. As the canyon developed into a metropolis and the Great Houses shot up to four and five stories, the walls got thicker, with wider cores, to support the additional weight. Upper level floors and roofs were composed of logs, branches, and mud.

This period of rapid growth lasted for some 300 years. Then, about 1150 or shortly thereafter, construction slowed to a stop at Chaco Canyon. Chaco's zenith lasted from 850 to about 1150 A.D. During the 1200s Chaco Canyon began losing population, gradually at first and then rapidly by the end of the century. By the early 1300s Chaco was nearly deserted, increasingly inhabited by nomadic groups who stayed for a short time and then moved on. By the end of the 14th century Chaco had become a city of ghosts.

So what happened? Several factors seem to have been involved in the depopulation of Chaco Canyon. First was a series of severe droughts culminating in the devastating drought of the last part of the 13th century that further damaged already depleted resources, including food and wood supplies. By 1300 the Chacoans had harvested virtually every tree in a 50-mile radius around the canyon. The scarcity of resources led in turn to civil strife and possible warfare with competing tribes from the Plains and other surrounding areas, although so far little evidence of violence at Chaco has been uncovered. Another contributing factor may have been the arrival of a new religion based on Kachinas that challenged the old elite and their priests who ruled by their knowledge of astronomical events. Or possibly Chacoans just grew tired of the hierarchical power structure at Chaco and decided to leave, either individually or with their clan, in search of a freer, more independent life. The great diaspora saw many Chacoans migrate southeast to pueblos along the Rio Grande, from Taos Pueblo down to Isleta Pueblo near Albuquerque. Others went north into southwestern Colorado and southeastern Utah. Still others went west into Arizona near Kayenta and the Hopi Mesas or southwest to Zuni, Acoma, and Laguna. They left behind a city of stone that has survived, deserted, for more than 700 years.

Today, getting to Chaco Canyon is not an easy task. Chaco is not a roadside stop or a quick photo op. I'm talking about a 3-4 hour drive from Santa Fe, and a 2-3 hour drive from Albuquerque, depending on road conditions. The turn-off to the canyon is on Highway 550 near Nageezi, which is halfway between Cuba and Aztec, New Mexico. You take County Road 7900 South, then turn right on 7950, and drive a total of 16 miles, most of it unpaved. The unpaved portion is deeply rutted and especially dangerous in inclement weather, when an all-wheel-drive vehicle is recommended if not required. From Durango to the north, Chaco is a two-hour drive south on 550, a distance of about 100 miles.

Entering the canyon you will see majestic Fajada Butte off to the left and then the Gallo Campground on the right. The Visitor Center is about a mile further on the right, where permits to enter the canyon can be purchased. The Visitor Center is open from 9 a.m. to 5 p.m. daily. At this writing, permits cost $25 per vehicle and $15 for each adult and are good for seven days. Senior and Access passes are honored. The trails and archaeological sites in the canyon are open daily from 7 a.m. to 5 p.m. November through February; 7 a.m. to 7 p.m. March through April; and 7 a.m. to 9 p.m. May through October. At sunset the entrance gate on the 8-mile Chaco Loop is closed and locked, so be sure you're out by sunset or you may end up spending the night with the ghosts of Chaco. The park is closed on Thanksgiving, Christmas Eve, Christmas Day, New Year's Eve, and New Years Day.

Gallo Campground

You'll find that Gallo Campground provides a convenient base of operations while you're at Chaco Canyon, especially if you decide to camp for a night or so. When I'm hiking at Chaco, I'm constantly taking photographs. Over the years I've taken thousands of photos, most of which I haven't processed. My point here is that it is extremely difficult to take all the photos you want in one day, so if you want to do extensive photographing, it would be wise to book a campsite at Gallo. You can hike the all the trails I mention here in two days.

If you are planning to camp at Chaco, here are a few things you should know about the campground. Gallo Campground is small with only 32 individual campsites, and is generally booked solid from May through October. Reservations are required and can be made at the Recreation.gov website. The fee at the time this book was published is $20 per night, $10 per night for seniors with Senior or Access cards. Campers should check in with the park ranger at the entrance to Gallo before proceeding. Arrival time is noon, and departing campers must be out by 11 a.m. the next day. Maximum length of stay is fourteen days.

Two group campsites are available, each accommodating up to thirty people and five vehicles. Group stays are limited to seven days. The group rate is $60 per might. Group sites are designed for tent camping and can't accommodate RVs. One campsite, 16, is designated as handicapped accessible, although I think most of the tent sites are equally accessible, as are the restroom facilities. You can check photos of the sites online at the Recreation.gov website to get a view of each site's layout.

Each campsite has a picnic table, fire grate, and tent pad made of sand. Restroom facilities are generally good, with running water and sinks for basic hygiene. All campsites come with parking spaces for one or two vehicles adjoining the site, which makes setting up camp fast and easy.

What I love about the campground is the quiet. Maybe it's my imagination, but Chaco campers tend to be of the reflective sort anyway, not the wild party animals you find at some other more easily accessible campgrounds. Only once in all my stays at Gallo have I encountered a loud, rambunctious group of teenagers with little parental control. You can pretty much count on a quiet evening and a good night's sleep.

Stop 1: Red Pictograph

Let's start at the campground, even if you aren't planning on camping for the night. You'll see the tents and RVs off to your right as soon as you enter the canyon. Drive through the campground and park near the Campfire Circle at the northern edge of Gallo. You'll see a large red pictograph on the cliff wall that marks the western border of the campground, just a short walk from your vehicle. This is my first photo stop, a shockingly bright ochre red pictograph that displays both animal and human figures, as well as instruments of one kind or another. Other symbols seem to depict fires or eruptions. The animals include a splayed bird, possibly a turkey, and a four-legged creature that resembles a big-horn sheep. One of the human figures seems to unravel, becoming a migration symbol. Two other human figures seem to be facing off, engaged in a heated discussion or even combat, with their arms waving about wildly.

What makes this pictograph so striking is its deep red color that, in the right light, seems to leap off the cliff. To capture this phenomenon, try taking photos early to mid morning, when the sun is high enough to bathe the entire cliff-face in light. The sunlight ignites the pictograph in a fiery blaze of red. If you stare at the pictograph too long, the figures seem to move. Or maybe that's just my imagination.

Here I would avoid afternoon or evening sessions. The pictograph needs the brilliant New Mexico light to come alive. I usually photograph this close up with a fixed lens for a sharper image and limited depth of field (basically, distance detail).

Pictograph in Gallo Campground.

Stop 2: Overlook Trail

From the pictograph, let's walk back to the entrance of Gallo Campground. You'll see a sign off to your right marking the Overlook Trail. An easy hike, the trail climbs up North Mesa and tracks along the edge of the cliff. When you reach the top, the view will take your breath away. Looking south, you'll see an enormous panorama of receding mesas rising up out of the high desert terrain, some as far away as Hosta Butte over forty miles southwest of Chaco. Straight ahead you look down on the majestic Fajada Butte. To your left: Chacra Mesa, directly east of Chaco. To your right: glimpses of South and West mesas, the two mesas that along with North Mesa encircle and protect the canyon.

The view is spectacular from anywhere on the Overlook Trail. Below on the floor of the canyon you'll see Chaco Wash winding its way through the entire length of the canyon, from Chacra Mesa east of the canyon all the way to West Mesa, behind which Chaco Wash merges with the Escavada Wash to form the Chaco River at the Convergence. More on the Convergence later.

My favorite spot on the trail comes at about the half-mile point. You'll find a rocky promontory jutting out over the lip of the cliff. From this rock you can photograph the entire vista with a wide-angle lens. The colors are intriguing: pink and gray cliffs, reddish brown buttes, and smoky green sage and saltbush. Or you can use a zoom lens to increase depth of field as you zero in on one particular mesa or stone ruin in the canyon. I never get tired of photographing Fajada Butte, famous for its so-called Sun Dagger, a configuration of sandstone rocks on the side of Fajada. The sandstone rocks cast shadows of the late morning and midday sun on a pictograph at certain times of the year, namely the solstice and equinox.

Why Fajada? Because the butte itself performs as a giant touchstone, a barometer of light and natural conditions at any given moment. No two photos of Fajada are ever alike, because the angle of light changes with the time of day and the location of the sun in the sky. When the light is angled, interesting shadows appear in the nooks and crannies of the massive rock. The steeper the angle, the longer the shadow. When the sun is low and in the southern sky, an entire side of Fajada remains in shadow, as in the photograph that follows.

I generally rely on my camera's automatic settings when using my zoon lens, which I always use on Fajada. The top brand cameras today are very, very sophisticated. However, I do bring a portable tripod with me at all times, so that if my camera's not offering me what I want, I'll change to manual. For example, if I want more depth of field, I'll set the camera on its highest F-stop (the higher the F-stop, the smaller the aperture, the deeper the depth of field--it's counterintuitive) and let the camera set the shutter speed accordingly.

Here's one of my photos of Fajada. Notice the angle of light. See if you can guess the sun's location in the sky.

Fajada Butte from the Overlook Trail.

Other photo opportunities at Gallo Campground: If you're camping at Gallo, check out the sunrise over Chacra Mesa to the east. It's often spectacular. Same with the sunsets behind North Mesa to the west. Also, if you're a fan of night photography, you've come to the right place. Because of the absence of light in Chaco Canyon, the skies are perfect for night photography. You can take photos from the campground or from the parking lot of the Visitor Center just a mile further down the road into the canyon. Or, better yet, you can walk down a sidewalk from the Visitor Center to Una Vida, the first small ruin in the canyon. The ruins can be a bit spooky after dark, but if you're desperate for a photo of Chaco's star-lit night skies and don't mind a little ghostly company, the Una Vida ruin is perfect.

Here's a photo of Fajada Butte I took at sunset from the Visitor Center parking lot using my zoom lens with flash.

Fajada Butte at sunset.

Downtown Chaco

Stop No. 3: Pueblo Bonito

Before entering the canyon proper, you'll need to stop at the Visitor Center for a permit. The Visitor Center is about a mile down the road on your right. As mentioned earlier, the fee is $25 per vehicle and $15 for each adult. Then it's on to the Chaco Loop, an eight-mile, one-way road that allows access to all the ruins in the canyon. In addition to the tiny Una Vida, you'll find six other Great Houses located on the canyon floor in what I call Downtown Chaco: Hungo Pavi, Chetro Ketl, Pueblo Bonito, Pueblo del Arroyo, Kin Kletso, and Casa Chiquita.

I usually stop first at the Pueblo Bonito parking lot, which provides trails to both Pueblo Bonito and Chetro Ketl. Pueblo Bonito (Spanish for "Beautiful Town") is the largest Great House at Chaco with over 650 rooms in what at one time was a sprawling, multi-storied structure built close to the North Mesa cliff. Because of its size and its location against the cliff, Bonito presents almost unlimited possibilities for photographing. As you walk around the D-shaped structure, every step you take offers a different view of Bonito and its relation to both the North Mesa and the expansive canyon.

Bonito Corners.

So even on a clear day you have to make choices. Where do you photograph? The entrances, the plazas, the interior rooms, or the massive rear wall? Or possibly the ramp walkway at the eastern end of Bonito that provides high ground and an unlimited view of the Great House and the canyon beyond. The walkway was built after a portion of the North Mesa cliff above Bonito collapsed in 1941 destroying about thirty rooms. I usually start with a long photo that shows or situates Bonito's position in the canyon. For this I've tried all my lenses, depending on what I wanted to highlight: Bonito in the foreground, the canyon in the background, or both. The walkway at the east end of Bonito works well for whatever choice you make. Here's a photo from the ramp that does both, showing portions of Bonito as well as Pueblo del Arroyo, Chaco Wash, and West Mesa in the distance.

Pueblo Bonito from the ramp walkway at its eastern end.

Then there's the sunlight factor. When the angle of light is low, and especially on cloudy or overcast days, Bonito and the other Great Houses are steeped in dark shadows. Ancient ruins engulfed in dark shadows can seem ominous, threatening, even a bit frightening. Lots of ghost stories have come out of Chaco Canyon--I've told a few myself. If you visit any of the larger Great Houses on an overcast day, you'll see what I mean. Take a look at this photo of Bonito, a side view with angled light.

Angled light producing dark shadows on Pueblo Bonito.

Taking photographs of the interior of Pueblo Bonito is a different thing entirely. For these I sometimes use the flash on my camera, especially when I'm trying to capture the nooks and crannies that you find everywhere in the Great Houses. Underground rooms are equally difficult. I've tried different lenses inside the rooms, with mixed results. For a sharper image I use my fixed lenses, which are better in low light situations, but if I want to frame the photo and photograph from a longer distance (and increase the depth of field), I will use my zoom lens with flash if necessary. With these photos I am more concerned with the effect I want than the fine detail.

The masonry in most of the rooms at Pueblo Bonito is incredibly sophisticated. The Chacoans built their dwellings with sandstone from the surrounding cliffs. The walls are built in what's called core-and-veneer construction, where a core of rubble and mud fills the space between two walls of chipped and fitted stones. Lower level walls have thicker cores so as to hold the weight of the floors and roofs above. There are five types of core-and-veneer masonry at Chaco Canyon, I through IV and McElmo, with MeElmo being the latest and most primitive. Types II, III, and IV are the most sophisticated, involving more of a pattern in the stones used, with repeating bands of small and large stones, almost like a rug or basket weaving.

Most of the Great Houses have a mix of types, relating to different stages of development. Types III and IV are the most intricate.

Here are two photos of lower level rooms in Pueblo Bonito, for which I used my zoom lens for better depth of field.

Lower rooms in Pueblo Bonito.

Lower doors in Pueblo Bonito.

Other photo opportunities: Pretty much everywhere you look at Pueblo Bonito, but pay close attention to the famous T-shaped doors, which are unique to Chaco. Also take a look at the massive rear wall that stabilizes the back of the Great House. The kivas, too, make for great photo opportunities. Chacoans lived in the small kivas; the larger or Great Kivas were for public ceremonies.

STOP NO. 4: CHETRO KETL

You can take the trail behind Pueblo Bonito to Chetro Ketl (possibly a rough translation of a Navajo word meaning 'Rain Pueblo'), the second largest Great House in the canyon at 500 rooms. The trail leads you to an incredible engineering achievement. The longest part of the rear wall of Chetro Ketl extends for an astounding 450 feet. Not only that, but the wall is for all intents and purposes perfectly plumb. After one thousand years! When I photograph this wall, I always use my zoom lens because I want the depth of field that reveals the magnitude of this wall. You can photograph from different locations, depending on what you want to include in the photo: the cliff of North Mesa, portions of the Great House, or even the larger canyon beyond the ruin.

Here's my take, using my zoom lens.

Rear wall of Chetro Ketl.

For close-ups, you can find wonderful windows, niches, and openings of one kind or another on the long rear wall. It's a photographer's delight. When you're finished, walk west around to the front of the Great House. You'll come to one of the enduring mysteries of Chaco Canyon: the Colonnade Architecture on the front wall of Chetro Ketl. Known for its columns, this architecture was common in the Toltec culture of Central Mexico (about 700–1000) but doesn't exist anywhere else in Chaco or its outliers. You can't help but notice the long, narrow room at the front of the Great House with its row of columns looking out on the plaza area. Apparently the columns were added around 1100, late in the construction of Chetro Ketl. The influence of Mesoamerica? The answer would seem to be yes, given the presence in Chaco of Macaws, cacao, sea shells, and precious stones from Mexico and Central America.

Now that you're in front of Chetro Ketl, notice the Plaza area is raised about twelve feet off the canyon floor. The Chacoans raised the Plaza by hand, carrying load after load of dirt and rock. An amazing feat, similar to the back wall of Chetro Ketl.

Further east, you'll find the famous Great Kiva of Chetro Ketl, the second largest Great Kiva at Chaco. Only Casa Rinconada is larger. Great Kivas contain the same formalized features, including an entryway and antechamber on the Plaza level, a low stone bench encircling the room, and a raised fire box and floor vaults for storage, presumably for ceremonial costumes and other paraphernalia. The Great Kiva offers endless opportunities for photos. Here's one of mine, where I've used shadows to highlight the interior of the Great Kiva. Here my zoom lens gives me the depth of field to situate the Great Kiva against North Mesa in the background.

Great Kiva of Chetro Ketl.

If you walk into the heart of Chetro Ketl, you'll come across an excavated room from the Great House's lower level. The view is fascinating, with a partial roof beam visible, as well as some sort of corner niche and other openings in the sandstone walls. The corner niche doesn't appear to be a door and can't very well be a window, so what was its purpose? An altar of some sort? Or perhaps only a niche for storage?

Excavated underground room in Chetro Ketl.

Other photo opportunities at Chetro Ketl: Take a look at the columns in front of Chetro Ketl. I've tried for years to get a good photo of the colonnade architecture, but I've never managed to find the right conditions and settings to get enough contrast between what's left of the columns and the rest of the Great House, never quite what I'm looking for. Maybe you will have better success. Another possibility: the balconies built on Chetro Ketl's rear wall facing the box canyon to the northeast of the ruin. Also, look closely as you hike along the cliff behind the Great House and you might see faint steps carved into the sandstone and small holes, or handholds, along the sides of the stairs. Lots to see, lots to photograph.

North Mesa

Stop No. 5: Kin Kletso

After you finish with Pueblo Bonito and Chetro Ketl, get back on the Chaco Loop and drive down to the end of the road at the Pueblo del Arroyo parking lot. West of the parking lot you'll see an old Navajo wagon road that becomes the West Mesa Trail. More on that later. For now, you might want to take a break at the picnic tables at the trailhead. Maybe lunch or just refreshments, either way it's a good place to stop for a break. It's even in the shade!

After your break, you have three choices. You can begin the long trek to West Mesa, you can walk up a small rise to the Kin Kletso Great House and climb the ancient stairway to North Mesa, or you can first visit Pueblo del Arroyo south of the road. Let's do Pueblo del Arroyo first, because it's small and takes only a few minutes.

A smaller Great House of 300 rooms, Pueblo del Arroyo is unique in that it is the only Great House in the interior of the canyon not backed up against North Mesa. Instead, it is located along Chaco Wash on the canyon floor, where presumably it monitored and protected Chaco's irrigation system. If you do walk through the ruin you will notice partial tri-walls. These are the only tri-walls in Chaco Canyon.

Now let's head to North Mesa. You first walk up to Kin Kletso (Navajo for 'Yellow House'). It's a small rectangular Great House of only 65 rooms. More important for hikers and photographers, it's where we catch the ancient Chacoan stairway up to North Mesa. For whatever reason, Kin Kletso always looks dark and foreboding. Maybe it's the primitive McElmo masonry as compared with the more sophisticated masonry in Pueblo Bonito and Chetro Ketl. Maybe it's the broken walls or the dark shadows cast by the tallest of the walls. Judge for yourself. I usually photograph this with my zoon lens so I can get the entire canyon in the background and good depth of field.

A spooky Kin Kletso.

Now follow a narrow trail behind Kin Kletso to a stand of boulders that serve as stepping-stones up the lower half of the trail. Then the trail reappears as a series of steps cut out of the soft sandstone. The steps take you up between a narrow gap in the cliff. Beware of slipping on the stones, which can be slippery if any moisture is present. Fortunately the gap in the cliff is narrow enough to allow you to hold on to both sides. When you reach the top and step out into the bright sunshine, the entire canyon will open up before you, a photographer's paradise. The view of the canyon from the top of North Mesa is simply magnificent.

View of Kin Kletso from Ancient Stairway.

Stop No. 6: Pueblo Bonito Overlook

The trail on top of North Mesa is clearly designated by cairns and occasional wooden signs. It takes you east along the cliff, passing by a series of sea fossils from when Chaco was under water during the Cretaceous Period, past pecked basins that were used by the Chacoans as receptacles for offerings, and past stone circles used for ancient ceremonies. After about a mile you will find yourself approaching the Pueblo Bonito overlook, a great place to take photos of Bonito and the canyon. Viewed from above, you see the enormity of the ruin, the geometrical patterns of the rooms and kivas, and the straight north-south wall cutting through the center of Bonito. Be careful, though. Don't get too close to the canyon rim. Much of the rock is loose or splitting from the cliff.

I use my zoom lens here in order to capture the entire canyon in great detail. However, I have taken photos of the interior of Pueblo Bonito with fixed lenses when I want to highlight a certain element: for example, the two plazas and their Great Kivas divided by a north-south wall. I've also used fixed lenses to photograph the oldest rooms in Pueblo Bonito on the right side of the photo, including Room 33 where a National Geographic Expedition in 1921 discovered fourteen burials of individuals believed to have been Chaco's ruling elite buried with tens of thousands of turquoise beads and pendants, as well as large quantities of shell and jet, flutes, ceremonial staffs, and conch shell trumpets. Next door in Room 28 archaeologists discovered 111 cylindrical jars with traces of cacao from Mesoamerica. Call it the Mesoamerican wing of Bonito!

Here's a long-lens photo of Pueblo Bonito and the canyon.

Pueblo Bonito from the Pueblo Bonito Overlook on the North Mesa Trail.

When you finish snapping photos, you can return to the trail and head due north on the remnants of the Great North Road. Segments of this road, the Chacoan version of a freeway, are thirty feet wide. Eventually you will come to a sign marking another Chacoan stairway, where the steps are carved out of the sandstone ridge. Once you get beyond this ridge, Pueblo Alto is clearly visible on the northern horizon, straight ahead. The small New Alto Great House is visible about 200 yards to the left of Alto.

Depending on the time of year, you might notice cactus flowers and other blooming plants as you walk up the road. I've taken interesting photos here, photographing close up with one of my two fixed lenses to blur the background.

Here's a photo of the Great North Road as you head back down into the canyon from Pueblo Alto, again taken with my long zoom lens for depth of field.

Chaco's Great North Road leading into the canyon.

From Pueblo Alto, the northernmost Great House in the canyon, the Great North Road extends from Alto all the way to Kurtz Canyon and possibly beyond to Salmon Ruins in Bloomington, New Mexico, and Aztec Ruins in Aztec, New Mexico. Fire towers have been discovered along the Great North Road that would enable a line- of-sight communication system to connect with northern outliers in places as distant as Chimney Rock, Colorado, near Pagosa Springs. Not only the Great North Road, but a maze of ancient roads branch out in pretty much every direction from Alto. The ancient roads have been mapped by means of aerial photography and, more recently, by lidar, and can be viewed online with a simple Google search.

Stop No. 7: Pueblo Alto

Pueblo Alto ('High Town' in Spanish) has 130 rooms and 18 small kivas. It's unique in two ways: it was only one story, and it does not have a Great Kiva. For me, only it's location on the Great North Road makes Pueblo Alto interesting. The ruin has never been reconstructed, so it lacks the kind of star power that Pueblo Bonito and Chetro Ketl display. It's mixed masonry styles look primitive in comparison, unfinished. Still, I like to photograph Pueblo Alto from its midden (or trash heap) on the eastern side of the ruin. I use a fixed lens and then crop the photo.

Pueblo Alto on the Great North Road.

If you continue walking north on the Great North Road you will come to the ruins of Rabbit Run. My advice would be to skip Rabbit Run, which is mostly a pile of stones and not particularly engaging visually. Instead, take the trail behind Pueblo Alto that loops southeast across the mesa. You'll find wild and interesting views of the mesa and the surrounding canyon from up here. Eventually you come to another ancient stairway. From there the trail curves south along the canyon behind Chetro Ketl and then west to the Chetro Ketl Overlook, another location where you can take spectacular photos.

Stop No. 8: Chetro Ketl Overlook

You have to make some choices here, because the sprawling Great House offers endless possibilities for snapping photos. You'll find it hard to get all of the intriguing features of Chetro Ketl in one frame and still get the detail you want. You have to choose what to include: the massive rear wall, the large Great Kiva, or the imposing block of rooms on the western side of the Great House. The expansive view of the canyon makes it even more difficult to choose, especially when you have an interesting array of clouds in the sky. Cloudy days are rare at Chaco, so when I'm there on a cloudy day I try to take advantage of the clouds. Here's an example. For this photograph I wanted to highlight Chetro Ketl's position in the canyon and under the cloudy sky. Using my zoom lens, I was able to capture the Great Kiva on the raised plaza and the block of rooms on the western side, as well as a slice of the rear wall. Notice the Great House occupies only about a third of the photo; the larger two-thirds I've given to the canyon and the sky. Again, the canyon itself is magnificent.

Cheto Ketl Overlook with clouds.

After you leave the Chetro Ketl Overlook, it's just a short hike straight ahead back to the ancient stairway behind Kin Kletso. On the way you can enjoy views of the wider canyon, the receding mesas that seem to touch the sky and the subtle colors of the cliffs, grays and pinks and browns. Notice, also, the fossils and large water basins on top of the cliffs, which the Chacoans used to catch rainwater whenever it chanced to rain, a rare occurrence in the arid Four Corners area. While you walk on the trail, shadows move across the floor of the canyon below, reflecting the movement of clouds across the sun. You can feel the wind and the movement of the cosmos. The canyon is alive and moving around you with birds in the sky and unseen, mostly nocturnal animals hidden in their burrows. Notice also the smoky green yucca, ocotillo, prickly pear, sage, saltbush and rabbitbush growing on the mesa. If you enjoy canyon hiking, this is as good as it gets.

STOP NO. 9: NORTH MESA VIEW

Wider view of Chaco Canyon from North Mesa.

When you're back at the Arroyo del Pueblo parking lot, you can once again rest at the shaded picnic tables. It's difficult to hike both the North Mesa Trail and the West Mesa Trail in the same day, so if you're camping at the Gallo Campground that night, you can postpone West Mesa until the following day. Instead, drive around the Chaco Loop and check out Casa Rinconada, the largest Great Kiva in Chaco Canyon. Then you can continue on to Gallo and set up camp, if you haven't already.

Other photo opportunities on North Mesa: For additional sites, check out Rabbit Run and the scattering of smaller ruins around Pueblo Alto. Most are no more than a crumbled wall, but Rabbit Run at least does offer some exceptional views of the Great North Road as it tails out into the mesas to the north of Chaco Canyon. Some interesting photos there.

West Mesa

The West Mesa Trail begins at the Pueblo del Arroyo parking lot, same as the North Mesa Trail. You walk past the Kin Kletso Great House on the old Navajo wagon road, which runs along Chaco Wash directly west. Chaco Wash itself is scenic, with willow and tamarisk growing on its banks, especially in Fall when the wash becomes a riot of color. Partly because of this, October is my favorite time to photograph in Chaco Canyon.

About a mile down the old wagon road you'll come to Casa Chiquita (Spanish for 'small house'), a small ruin on the far side of Clys Canyon. Old Schoolers will remember Clys Canyon as the previous entrance to Chaco Canyon, where N.M. State Road 57 came plunging down the canyon wall. It was quite a sight back in the early 1970s, when I first started coming to Chaco. Back then you could drive or walk virtually anywhere in the canyon and rarely saw another visitor. Today, I would skip the visually unremarkable Casa Chiquita and continue on to Chaco's famous petroglyph panels about three-fourths of a mile further.

Stop No. 10: Petroglyph Panels

The Petroglyph Trail branches off the main trail and takes you up to the North Mesa cliff, where you'll find six panels of petroglyphs carved into the sandstone cliff. These represent the largest collection of petroglyphs at Chaco Canyon. The panels are fun to photograph and even more fun trying to 'read'. As I mentioned before, some aficionados claim to be able to read Native American pictographs and petroglyphs, seeing the panels as texts composed of symbols.

Here's Panel 4, photographed with a fixed lens for a sharper image. The three figures in the panel seem to be a bighorn sheep, a human being, and some sort of katsina mask possibly representing a supernatural being. The story? How about a narrative: the katsina helps the human kill the sheep? Or perhaps a statement (since the katsina is foregrounded and both human and sheep are distant background images): the katsina controls both human and animal kingdoms? Whatever.

Petroglyph Panel 4.

Stop No. 11: Supernova Pictograph

Go back to the main trail and continue walking west. As you approach West Mesa the trail turns left and crosses Chaco Wash, which is usually dry. However, on several occasions I've found standing water in the wash and had to be careful winding my way across the wash searching for dry ground. So be mindful crossing the wash. Once you reach the far bank the trail begins to cut back and forth up the mesa. A half-mile or so further you will come to a marked spur trail to the right. This short spur will take you to our next photo stop: a shallow overhang along the cliff wall painted with pictographs. On the ceiling you will see pictographs of a star, a crescent moon, and a human hand. Many people think this star pictograph is a representation of the 1054 supernova (or exploding star) that would have been visible in the sky over Chaco for twenty days and visible at night for nearly two years. Others are understandably skeptical of the supernova theory. I would generally be skeptical of a claim like this, but since all the ruins in Chaco are aligned to both lunar and solar events or considerations, I remain undecided.

I've snapped photos of this overhang using both fixed and zoom lenses, trying to get the best photo possible. Here's one I took with a fixed lens. Notice the wasp next in the lower left corner.

Supernova Pictograph.

When you return to the main trail, you'll find it's a steep climb to the Peñasco Blanca Great House high on West Mesa. Spanish for 'white cliff' or 'white bluff', Peñasco Blanco sits perched on the very top of West Mesa, overlooking the entire length of the canyon to the east and the Convergence of Chaco Wash and Escavada Wash to the west (more on this later). Peñasco Blanco was one of the earliest Great Houses built at Chaco, with three stories and 215 rooms. Construction started about 850, about the same time as initial construction began on Pueblo Bonito.

Stop No. 12: Peñasco Blanco

Peñasco Blanco is essentially unexcavated. Isolated, the Great House is untouched, except by time. Whereas most of the other Great Houses get lots of visitors, Peñasco Blanco gets very few. No doubt this is partly due to its remoteness and to the difficulty of the hike up West Mesa. That suits me fine, because up on top of West Mesa looking down at the canyon or the convergence is the only place in Chaco where I still feel the sense of a presence. I can't define it any more than that: just a presence. Back in the 1970s when I first started coming to Chaco Canyon, I saw very few other people but lots of pottery shards everywhere in the canyon. Today the pottery shards are all gone, picked clean by the masses of visitors who come to Chaco every year. And so is the presence I once felt pretty much everywhere in the canyon. This is the reason I like to hike up to Peñasco Blanco: to revisit that presence.

Here's a photo of Peñasco Blanco as you approach the top of West Mesa. For this photo I use my zoom lens. For photographing inside the Great House, I use a fixed lens.

Approaching Peñasco Blanco.

As I say, I like to spend some time at Peñasco Blanco. You can explore the Great Kivas and search for Chacoan Road segments that entered the canyon here from the west. In fact, the southern-most Great Kiva at Peñasco

Blanco is adjacent to a 30-foot wide Chacoan road segment. The view to the east is spectacular. You can see the entire length of the canyon and the various Great Houses built against North Mesa. From high on North Mesa, the canyon looks like a grand boulevard, along which the massive Great Houses have been built. The view to the west is just as magnificent: buttes, mesas, and the Chuska Mountains.

It's also, I should add, a perfect place to watch the sun move east to west and to measure the sun's angle in the sky, as it deceases from Summer to Winter Solstice and then expands from Winter to Summer Solstice.

Inside Peñasca Blanco.

Stop No. 13: The Convergence

When you finish at Peñasco Blanco, you'll find the hike down the mesa a lot easier than the hike up. The breather usually gives me enough energy for the next and last part of this hike: the Convergence of the Chaco and Escavado washes to form the Chaco River. Once you reach Chaco Wash at the base of West Mesa, just follow it west as it circles behind West Mesa. The wash narrows here and often has at least some standing water, which can make it a muddy hike. But the view of the Convergence is well worth the difficulty.

Here's a zoom photo of Chaco Wash as it narrows approaching the Convergence. Notice the pools of water in the bottom of the wash.

Chaco Wash entering the Convergence.

Entering the Convergence always reminds me of that scene in The Wizard of Oz movie where Dorothy wakes up in Oz and the movie switches from black and white to living color. The shift is that abrupt. Startling really. You walk into a vast river of white sand, fifty to one hundred yards wide, dry as a bone. It's one of the hidden treasures of Chaco Canyon, a place where few hikers ever venture.

Sounds crazy, but the bed of the Convergence resembles a beach, with fine white sand and dunes. Call it Chaco Canyon's waterworks. Lidar has found evidence of Chacoan dams, terraces, and ponds at the Convergence. There is even evidence that the ponds were used for recreational purposes. Go figure.

The brilliant white sand and surrounding mesas make it an exciting place to photograph. What's more, I've found horses grazing on the sandy bottom each time I've visited the Convergence. Since the Convergence borders the Navajo Reservation, the horses could belong to the Navajo families who live in the area. Or the horses could be wild. At any rate the equines always go about their business grazing, ignoring the funny two-legged creature pursing them with a black object on his face.

I always take photos with my zoom lens here, for obvious reasons. The depth of field is a requirement.

Convergence of the Chaco and Escavada washes.

Save some time for the hike back to the Pueblo del Arroyo parking lot, a good four miles. Once you get back to the parking lot, you have some choices to make. If you're on a day visit, you probably only have time for one more stop. Again, I would recommend Casa Rinconada, the largest Great Kiva at Chaco. Plus, the Casa Rinconada parking lot is right on the Chaco Loop. You can stop on your way out of the park.

Stop No. 14: Casa Rinconada

Follow the Chaco Loop across the bridge over Chaco Wash and around to the next pull-off. You'll see Casa Rinconada on the hill above. As I mentioned, Casa Rinconada is a monster, the largest excavated Great Kiva at Chaco and one of the largest in the entire Southwest, with an average diameter of 63 feet. Remember, Great Kivas were used for ceremonial and religious events. This public function explains some of the intriguing features of Casa Rinconada. For example, if you look carefully you'll see that both the north and south entryways were connected to anterooms that lead into the kiva. The north entry in particular had six rooms attached to its anteroom and then a 39-foot underground passage, 3 feet deep and 3 feet wide, leading into the kiva. You can imagine public ceremonies with dancers, priests, or kachinas (people dressed as gods) entering the kiva through this passage to perform for the members of the gathered clan.

Inside Casa Rinconada you see the typical features shared by all kivas, including a firebox, masonry vaults, and intermittent niches built into the wall of the kiva. A stone bench for sitting encircles the underground structure, large enough to accommodate dozens of celebrants. Stone stairways lead into the north and south antechambers from which the priests or dancers would emerge. And four large seating pits for roof supports are clearly visible. The supports would have been massive logs cut from forests as far away as fifty miles. The kiva roof would have been constructed with the same materials used for roofs in the Great Houses: wood beams overlaid with willow branches and then layered with mud and juniper bark.

Casa Rinconada.

Other photograph opportunities on West Mesa: The Convergence is one of Chaco's hidden treasures. The white sand, the dunes, the rocky mesas on all sides of the Convergence, and of course the horses grazing on the bottom of riverbed, totally oblivious to all human activity. You could spend hours here, exploring and taking photos.

South Mesa

If you have time, or are enjoying your second day at Chaco, consider hiking up South Mesa. It doesn't offer the same kind of attractions that North Mesa and West Mesa offer, but you will find one Great House, Tsin Kletsin, protecting the southern entrance to the canyon. The trail up South Mesa begins at Casa Rinconada. It leads sharply to the west and then cuts back as you begin to climb South Mesa. It's a long, gradual ascent that takes longer than you think, primarily because the trail is quite steep in some places and littered with loose rocks. Also, the trail is not as clearly marked by cairns as most of the other trails in the canyon, so it's easy to lose track of the route. My guess is that the trail isn't particularly well tended because relatively few visitors hike up to South Mesa.

This is a shame, because South Mesa offers some of the best views of the canyon and its surroundings. The view of the canyon as you climb up South Mesa is spectacular. Pueblo Bonito and Chetro Ketl stand directly across the canyon from the trail. If you're like me, you'll find yourself looking back over your shoulder and stopping repeatedly to take photos. I can only imagine what it must have been like a thousand years ago to descend into this urban center of four- and five-story Great Houses. This view is the closest I'll ever come to understanding that feeling.

Stop No. 15: The Chaco Meridian

From the top of South Mesa you can see the rough North-South alignment of the ruins in Chaco Canyon, what Stephen Lekson calls the "Chaco Meridian" (about 108 degrees longitude). The "Chaco Meridian" bisects the canyon from Pueblo Alto on top of North Mesa down through Pueblo Bonito and Casa Rinconada on the floor of the canyon to Tsin Kletsin on top of South Mesa. Lekson argues in his book of the same name that the line had deep significance to the Chacoans, and when they abandoned Chaco around 1200, they moved first north to Aztec Ruins in northern New Mexico and later south to Pacquime in northern Mexico, always on the meridian.

Here is a zoom photo of the alignment in the canyon along the Chaco Meridian: Pueblo Alto, Pueblo Bonito, and Casa Rinconada. Tsin Kletsin would be directly behind the camera.

The Chaco Meridian.

Warning: If you manage to hike all the way to the top of South Mesa, you'll probably be disappointed, because Tsin Kletsin is not Pueblo Bonito or Chetro Ketl. Tsin Kletsin (Navajo for 'Black Wood Place') is a small 70-room Great House with McElmo style masonry that has been allowed to deteriorate over the centuries. Its three kivas and two enclosed plazas have never been excavated or stabilized. Several Chacoan road fragments have been found near Tsin Kletsin. One leads from Tsin Keltsin north to an ancient stairway down into the canyon. Still, if you make it to the top, the southernmost Great House in the canyon is worth a few photos, if only to show that you made it to the top of South Mesa.

Stop No. 16: Tsin Kletsin

Here's a photo of Tsin Kletsin taken with my zoon lens on a bright sunny day that makes the ruin look more inviting than it deserves.

Tsin Kletsin.

Other photo opportunities on South Mesa: The Chaco elk herd. Yes, Chaco has its own elk herd that numbers about twenty-five. They come down from South Mesa late every afternoon to graze and look for water in Chaco Wash. If you're around South Mesa in the late afternoon, get your camera ready. The elk are gorgeous creatures. What's more, these elk are used to humans gawking at them.

Wijiji Trail and Chacra Mesa

After South Mesa, there's only one more trail to explore, the Wijiji Trail along Chacra Mesa directly east of the campground. Unlike the other trails at Chaco, there's no parking lot for the hike east to Wijij (perhaps Navajo for 'Black Greasewood'). You can park in the marked pull-off along the road into Chaco just east of the campground. Or if you happen to be camping, you can leave your vehicle at the campground and hike over to the trailhead, an easy walk.

The trail to Wijiji, the easternmost Great House in the Park, runs alongside Chaco Wash and follows Chacra Mesa east. You'll notice how the wash has been affected by extensive arroyo cutting, which has carved out side channels and gullies that divert much needed water from the canyon floor. Arroyo cutting can be incredibly destructive to water movement and thus agriculture and could have contributed to the hard times that befell Chaco in the 12th century.

STOP NO. 17: CHACO WASH ARROYO CUTTING

However, arroyo cutting also makes for interesting photographs. You can see the damage erosion has done, leaving Chaco Wash a twisting and turning slash in the canyon floor. In places the sides of the wash have collapsed, forming mini dams that either block or direct the flow of water in random, unlikely directions. The resulting topsy-turvy landscape grows even more dramatic in the early Fall, when the leaves of the bushes and trees along Chaco Wash paint the rugged canyon floor in bright yellow and red colors.

Here's a zoom photo of the arroyo cutting and Fall colors on Chaco Wash looking back toward Fajada Butte, taken in October.

Fall colors on Chaco Wash.

Unlike the more rigorous trails at Chaco, the trail to Wijiji involves no climbing or difficult stretches. It's a flat, leisurely hike that allows for meditation. Along the way you can pause for photos of Chacra Mesa to the south or for a panorama photograph of the canyon behind you. From the trail you can see how the canyon opens up, with Fajada Butte and South Mesa to the left, and North Mesa to the right. The ruins of Pueblo Bonito and Chetro Ketl are just visible if you look closely. This is the view Chacoans would have had when entering the canyon from the east.

STOP NO. 18: WIJIJI

Wijiji (perhaps Navajo for 'Black Greasewood') seems to materialize out of the canyon wall to the north. In fact, its placement against the cliff wall makes an otherwise mundane Great House visually striking. Like Peñasco Blanco and Tsin Kletsin, it commands an entrance to the canyon. With two or three stories, Wijiji had a total of 225 rooms, 100 of them on the ground floor. Wijiji has the reputation of being the most symmetrical of Chacoan Great Houses, with two symmetrically placed kivas in its north room block and identical east and west wings.

Wijiji.

There are no Great Kivas in the ruin itself (though there is one about half a mile away) and not much evidence of residential use. For example, no trash midden has been found in the area. The speculation is that Wijiji was used for visitors, either traders or pilgrims arriving for calendrical religious ceremonies at Chaco. Wijiji has not been excavated.

I like to linger at Wijiji, poke around the ruin and the arroyo, snap some panoramic views of the canyon and look for trails leading up to the mesa tops. If you're patient you can find animal trails leading up North Mesa and Chacra Mesa especially, because Navajo sheepherders have a long history of grazing their herds on Chacra long after the Ancestral Puebloans abandoned the canyon.

Other photo opportunities on the Wijiji Trail: The arroyo cutting presents endless opportunities for photographs. Also, check out the red pictograph panel about 300 feet east of the ruin. Just follow the marked trail to an overhang in the cliff behind Wijiji. You'll find two red animal images surrounded by handprints. Another striking red image at Chaco, easy to photograph.

After you've finished at Wijiji, you will have photographed all the attractions I recommend. If you've only been at Chaco for an afternoon, or even if you've camped overnight, you might want to return for another visit. I think you will find that even if you come back and photograph the same sites from the same angles, no two photos will be the same: seasons change, weather conditions change, and the quality of the light changes at the blink of an eye. Chaco is always a new experience, no matter how many times you visit.

I can't count the number of days I've spent at Chaco. But I'm always looking forward to my next visit, excited about what new visual delights I will discover and photograph. I'm never disappointed. And when I leave Chaco Canyon after each visit, it's with a sense of wonder and amazement that, six hundred years before Europeans set foot on this continent, the Ancestral Puebloans created this monumental stone city.

After the Fall: A Short History

Contrary to popular belief, Chaco's rich history didn't end when the Ancestral Puebloans abandoned the canyon. The Navajo moved South into the Four Corners area sometime between 1400 and 1525 A.D. Some of the Navajo oral histories place their arrival much earlier, even overlapping with the Puebloan presence at Chaco. At any rate, the Navajo began herding sheep, goats, and horses in the greater Chaco area at least by the late 1500s near Chacra Mesa, Kin Klizhin and other sites around the canyon.

The Navajo occupation of the Chaco area was ongoing when the Spanish arrived in New Mexico in the late 16th century. Possibly, the first recorded Spanish contact with the Navajo took place in 1583 when an expedition led by Antonio de Espejo encountered what he described as "Indios Serranos" (Mountain Indians) near Mount Taylor on his way to Zuni Pueblo. Many of the official records of the Spanish entrance into New Mexico were destroyed during the Pueblo Revolt of 1680 when the Puebloans laid siege to Santa Fe and captured the *Casas Reales* (government buildings). A good many Navajo had joined the Puebloans during the uprising and then later given them shelter after the Spanish returned in 1692, which increased tensions between the Spanish and Navajo, who by this time had a considerable presence in Chaco Canyon.

During the 17th and 18th centuries, as the Spanish spread out into the Four Corners area, they competed with the Navajo for land and resources. The situation became even more complicated after 1846, when Gen. Stephen Watts Kearney arrived in Santa Fe and claimed the city and the territory for the United States. Soon both Spanish and Anglo ranchers were competing with the Navajo in and around Chaco. One Anglo ranch, the LC operation, was headquartered just North of Penasco Blanco; another, the Carlisle Cattle Co. was located on Gallegos Wash to the North.

Whereas the Navajo were a bit wary of the Chaco ruins, at times associating them with places like the "White House" in some of their migration stories where evil things were said to have occurred, the Anglos had no such reservations. The first explicit report of Chaco Canyon by an American was in 1849 by First Lt. James H. Simpson of the U.S. Army Topographical Engineers. Simpson measured and described seven major and several smaller ruins, giving them names provided by his guides, who were both Native American and Spanish. His reports created a national interest in Chaco Canyon and its spectacular ruins, but it wasn't until after the Civil War that adventurers began visiting the canyon, intrigued by articles appearing in the popular press.

Enter Richard Wetherill, a Colorado rancher, explorer, and amateur archaeologist (or looter, some would say). Wetherill was famous for finding the abandoned Cliff Palace at Mesa Verde in 1888 and organizing an excavation, during which they dug, catalogued, and gathered artifacts that were later sold to the Historical Society of Colorado.

By the time he arrived in Chaco a few years later, Wetherill was already something of a national celebrity. Wetherill secured funding from wealthy New Yorkers Talbot and Frederick Hyde, and in 1896 began excavations at Pueblo Bonito. The Hyde Exploring Expedition, under the direction of F.W. Putnam of the American Museum of Natural History and Harvard University, removed massive amounts of artifacts from Bonito that were sent east to the Hydes and the American Museum of Natural History. Today I think it's fair to say that most people believe these artifacts should have remained in Chaco or at least in New Mexico museums. I certainly do.

Curiously, Wetherill remained in Chaco, building a homestead and a trading post, which he named the Bonito Trading Post. In its first manifestation the trading post was a rather humble one-room stone structure built out from the rear wall of Pueblo Bonito. An 1897 photograph, ostensibly taken by Wetherill, shows the structure under construction. Wetherill later expanded the trading post, building a homestead and a much larger trading post southwest of Pueblo Bonito, which he ran from the late 1890s until his death in 1910. To be precise, Wetherill was shot and killed by a Navajo man for reasons that are somewhat murky. He and his wife Marietta are buried in the small, fenced cemetery northwest of Pueblo Bonito.

But Wetherill wasn't the only American who tried to commercialize Chaco. There were at least two other active trading posts in the canyon, Chaco Canyon Trading Post at Pueblo del Arroyo, and Kimbeto Trading Post above Escavada Wash just north of the canyon. The rush was on as ranchers, explorers and looters headed for the canyon. To prevent further looting or damage to prehistoric ruins, the United States Congress passed the Antiquities Act in 1906. The following year President Theodore Roosevelt created the "Chaco Canyon National Monument" on March 11, 1907, one of the first 18 national monuments created by Roosevelt.

In 1921 a National Geographic Society Expedition under the direction of Neil M. Judd, Curator of Archaeology at the United States National Museum, began excavating at Pueblo Bonito. By this time the science of dendrochronology for dating trees and other technological advances allowed for a more professional dig. During the excavation, the National Geographic Society funded preservation efforts to stabilize the ruin. It was the Judd team that discovered and catalogued the burials in Room 33, along with the thousands of turquoise beads, jewelry, seashells, and other ceremonial paraphernalia.

Also in 1921 another archaeologist, Edgar L. Hewett, began an excavation of Chetro Ketl. Over time Hewett created the Chaco Field School, a laboratory for archaeology students working at Chaco. Hewett's program was jointly run and funded by the School of American Research (now the School for Advanced Research) in Santa Fe and the University of New Mexico in Albuquerque. His students excavated over a hundred rooms at Chetro Ketl, finding similar, but fewer, precious stones and ceremonial paraphernalia than was found in Pueblo Bonito. In the 1930s Hewett and his students excavated Casa Rinconada and many other small one- and two- story dwellings in the canyon.

By the outbreak of World War II, Hewett's research station included a headquarters, a shop, a bathhouse, a photographic laboratory, storerooms, a dining room and kitchen, and eleven dormitories shaped like Navajo hogans. Back then Chaco had no visitor center. Instead, a caretaker was housed in a makeshift office near Pueblo Bonito. The first visitor center was built in 1957 as part of the "Mission 66" initiative to expand and upgrade national parks in the ten-year period leading up to the 50th anniversary of our national parks in 1966. The Chaco improvements included construction of a visitor center, housing for the staff, and a campground. In 2011 the visitor center was remodeled, with expanded museum exhibits, to its present form.

Over the last few decades there have been several major archaeology surveys and projects at Chaco, including the Chaco Project Archaeological Survey 1971–1975 by the Chaco Center, a joint venture of the U.S. Department of Interior, the National Park Service, and the University of New Mexico, and the follow-up Additional Lands Archaeological Survey 1983–1984. Both surveys have been digitalized by the Chaco Research Archive and are available online at chacoarchive.org. I should also mention the National Park Service's Chaco Project 1971–1986 and the Chaco Stratigraphy Project, which began in 2004, directed by Patricia Crown and Chip Wills.

The Chaco Solstice Project, directed by Anna Sofaer, began in 1978. Sofaer and her contributors analyzed astronomical alignments at Chaco Canyon. Among other things, they found that basically all Chacoan Great Houses were oriented to the cycles of the sun or moon. They also found that, geographically, the Great Houses were located along lines related to these solar and lunar cycles. Their work supports the theory that ceremonies commemorating these solar and lunar cycles unified Chacoan society and solidified the rule of an elite who had knowledge of these recurring rhythms in the sky over Chaco Canyon and used that knowledge to maintain power. The Solstice Project team also mapped the maze of Chacoan roads surrounding Pueblo Alto on the North Mesa by using Lidar (Light Detection and Ranging technology).

The same technology was used by Kenneth B. Tankersley of the University of Cincinnati Anthropology and Geology departments to map a bank of dunes near the convergence of the Chaco and Escavada washes. In a research article on Ancestral Puebloan water management in the *Journal of Archeologic Sciences*, Tankersley identifies images of dunes, canals, and reservoirs used by Chacoans as water management systems. No doubt Chaco will continue to yield more secrets as Lidar and other new technologies become more widely used in the canyon.

On December 19, 1980, Chaco Canyon National Monument experienced a name change, becoming the Chaco Culture National Historical Park. At the same time 13,000 additional acres were added to the park. In 1987 Chaco became a UNESCO World Heritage Site.

Chaco still retains much of its grandeur seven centuries after its fall. Looking back from the long view of history it's clear that Chaco was a way station, not only for individuals and clans, but for an entire culture passing through, searching for the Center Place after emergence. The migration symbols everywhere on the walls of the canyon tell the story. We are all passing through—this place, this time, this life. All of us, all of our families, have our own history of migration. Indeed, the story of humans on this planet is a story of migration. This is what Chaco means to me. This is why I love the canyon.

Recommended Reading

Carter, William B. *Indian Alliances and the Spanish in the Southwest, 750–1750*. Norman, Oklahoma: University of Oklahoma Press, 2009.

Crown, Patricia. *The House of the Cylinder Jars: Room 28 in Pueblo Bonito, Chaco Canyon*. Albuquerque, New Mexico: University of New Mexico Press, 2020.

Curry, Andrew. "DNA Offers Clues to Mysterious Crypt in Ancient Pueblo." Washington, DC: *National Geographic*, Feb. 21, 2017.

Goin, Peter, and Lucy R. Lippard. *Time and Time Again: History, Rephotography, and Preservation in the Chaco World*. Santa Fe, New Mexico: Museum of New Mexico Press, 2013.

Lekson, Stephen H. *The Chaco Meridian: One Thousand Years of Political and Religious Power in the Ancient Southwest*, Second Ed. New York: Rowman and Littlefield, 2015.

Lekson, Stephen H. *A History of the Ancient Southwest*. Santa Fe, New Mexico: School for Advanced Research Press, 2008.

Malville, J. McKim. *Guide to Prehistoric Astronomy in the Southwest*. Boulder, Colorado: Johnson Books, 2008.

Morrow, Baker H. and V.B. Price, eds. *Anasazi Architecture and American Design*. Albuquerque, New Mexico: University of New Mexico Press, 1997.

Plog, Stephen and Carrie Heitman. "Hierarchy and Social Inequality in the

American Southwest, A.D. 800–1200." Washington, DC: Proceedings of the National Academy of Sciences, *PNAS*, Nov.16, 2010,107(46) 19619-19626.

Roney, John R. "Prehistoric Roads and Regional Integration in the Chacoan System." In *Anasazi Regional Organization and the Chaco System*, edited by David E. Doyel, pp. 123-131. Papers of the Maxwell Museum of Anthropology 5. Albuquerque, NM: University of New Mexico Press, 1992.

Sofaer, Anna, ed. *Chaco Astronomy: An Ancient American Cosmology*. Santa Fe, New Mexico: Ocean Tree Books, 2007.

Tankersley, K.D. 2017. "Geochemical, Economic, and Ethnographic Approaches to the Evaluation of Soil, Salinity, and Water Management in Chaco Canyon, New Mexico." *Journal of Archaeologic Sciences: Reports* (April 2017) 12:378-383.

Wilson, James C. *Hiking New Mexico's Chaco Canyon: the Trails, the Ruins, the History*. Santa Fe, New Mexico: Sunstone Press, 2019.

www.ingramcontent.com/pod-product-compliance
Lightning Source LLC
Chambersburg PA
CBHW042340150426
43195CB00006B/118